Dying of the Light

Dying of the Light

A Poetry Collection

Kit Willett

RESOURCE *Publications* • Eugene, Oregon

DYING OF THE LIGHT
A Poetry Collection

Copyright © 2022 Kit Willett. All rights reserved. Except for brief quotations in critical publications or reviews, no part of this book may be reproduced in any manner without prior written permission from the publisher. Write: Permissions, Wipf and Stock Publishers, 199 W. 8th Ave., Suite 3, Eugene, OR 97401.

Resource Publications
An Imprint of Wipf and Stock Publishers
199 W. 8th Ave., Suite 3
Eugene, OR 97401

www.wipfandstock.com

PAPERBACK ISBN: 978-1-6667-5722-4
HARDCOVER ISBN: 978-1-6667-5723-1
EBOOK ISBN: 978-1-6667-5724-8

09/28/22

This collection is dedicated to Hilary and all those who challenge systems of power. In the face of adversity and hopelessness, may your courage and integrity lead you; when met with patronization, may your story and community bring you strength; when your voice is among those who do not value it, may you sing, clear and strong.

Thou wilt not leave me in the loathsom grave
His prey, nor suffer my unspotted Soule
For ever with corruption there to dwell;
But I shall rise Victorious, and subdue
My Vanquisher, spoild of his vanted spoile;
Death his deaths wound shall then receive, and stoop
Inglorious, of his mortal sting disarm'd.

—PARADISE LOST (3.247–53)

Contents

Preface | xi
Acknowledgements | xvii

Prologue
  At the Beginning of a Journey | 3

Act One
  Like Any Other Day | 7
  Why I Listen to Folk-Punk | 8
  Broken | 10
  Liberation I: Wrath | 11
  Liberation II: For a Moment | 12
  Trapped, Observed | 13
  Liberation III: Lest We Celebrate | 14

Act Two
  A Rare Scene | 17
  Ribbons and Naked Fabric | 18
  Disclosure | 19
  A Younger Sibling Appears | 20
  Wild Shelter | 21
  Canticle I: The Oasis | 22
  Creation Hymn | 24
  Dinner Plans | 25
  Hospitality | 26

Act Three

Finding Process | 29
Aroha Mai, Aroha Atu | 30
Bugle | 31
The Birth of Institutions | 32
A Bowl of Fruit | 33
Bricks Fall | 34
The Great Plot | 35
Baptized First in Blood | 36
Tough Love | 37
Alone Time | 38
Streetlight | 39
The Fall, Part One: Suspension | 40
The Fall, Part Two: Firmly Held | 41
The Fall, Part Three: Filthy Hands and Muddy Feet | 42
The Fall, Part Four: Resentment | 43
The Fall, Part Five: Taste the Fruit | 44

Act Four

Optimism | 49
Canticle II: A Grove | 50
Like That Other Day | 52
Death | 53
On a Bench, Observing a Bridge | 54
A Mountain Landscape | 55
Institutions | 56
Reflection | 57

Act Five

Future I: Cain and Abel | 61
Future II: Noah's Lullaby | 62
Future III: Overheard at a Seminary | 63

Surrender | 64
End | 66
Wood and Water | 67
Unlike Any Other Day | 68
Felix Culpa | 69

Epilogue
Onward: A Benediction | 73

Preface

My primary motivation behind writing this collection was two-fold: *Dying of the Light* should reframe Milton's *Paradise Lost* in a way that is sympathetic to Lucifer, and it should be proof of the generative nature of contemplative practices when applied to text. This project is the result of my Master of Creative Writing research, which I undertook in 2020; the poetry collection is the creative thesis, and this preface is a reduction of the collection's accompanying exegesis.

Reframing *Paradise Lost*

Its title comes from Dylan Thomas' 'Do not go gentle into that good night': a poem about the death of a father. The reference raised three provocations for me in writing: first, that we might need to 'rage against the dying' of Lucifer (Light Bringer); also, that we might need to explore the death of the metaphor of God as father: that patriarchal language obscures God; and, that the privileged—those for whom it is perhaps easy to 'go gently' or act passively in the world—might need to approach the hard work of deconstructing their privilege.

Toward the end of this collection, the 'śāṭān' is considered an oppositional role that is played by anyone who challenges homogeneity. The reasoning here is to assert the importance of otherness in society: it is just and necessary for us to encounter difference, and there is danger in people with religiopolitical power demonizing those who protest.

In retelling *Paradise Lost*, I felt a great tension between ideal and reality when exploring God, Jesus, and the church, and this tension is kept raw on the page; however, the discrepancies in the

Preface

depictions of God are deliberate. God becomes more gendered and toxic throughout act three as they begin to be perceived through a human lens, but the juxtaposition of a creative image of God and a destructive image is intended as a merism. God is expressed as being the entirety of the spectrum of creativeness and destructiveness. That is to say, God is not only both creative and destructive but also exists in the grey space between the two.

Contemplative Practices as Generative

Contemplative practices have long been used to make meaning from sacred texts. During the writing of this collection, I used a range of spiritual practices with *Paradise Lost* to glean its significant messages. I tried to approach every practice with reverence.

In undertaking this process, I found that the real-life experiences I was processing would wind up in the text I was reading as well as the text I was writing. Perhaps, therefore, a text we treat as sacred meets the needs of each reader.

I found these practices deeply rewarding in poetic generation but also in my personal spiritual growth, and I love this collection not only as a product but as a keepsake of a process.

These contemplative practices are from a range of traditions, and some of them have been adapted from their contexts by my Christocentric worldview. The following is an outline of the practices I used:

> **Benediction:** Adele Calhoun writes in Spiritual Disciplines Handbook that blessing desires to 'instill courage, confidence and hope through expressing the delight God has in others.' Benedictions tend to use an anaphoric 'may'; given their repetitive structure, they are not unlike existing writing prompts that demand a list of 'things you wish for someone'.
>
> **Florilegium:** Florilegium is the practice of flos-legere, or flower gathering. To practice this, you keep a journal of impactful phrases that are plucked from sacred texts like flowers. When laid together on the same page, these 'flowers' inform a new

Preface

and more significant meaning about the (often emotional) space the person collecting them is occupying.

Icon meditation: Reading icons is a particularly Eastern and Russian Orthodox practice and involves sitting with a sacred image and pondering what it can teach us about God. For this collection, I used a range of icons, including Blake's and Doré's illustrations of *Paradise Lost* and traditional Christian icons.

Ignatian contemplation: As far as sacred practices go, Ignatian contemplation (or sacred imagination) is quite simple: imagine yourself into the sacred text as a notable character or as a bystander, and, by sensorially experiencing the narrative, you gain new insights about the text or God.

Kashf: Kashf translates as 'unveiling'. It is a Sufi practice that asks the reader to approach the text with their heart instead of their head and allow the text to speak directly, rather than have a reader seek an interpretation.

Lectio Divina: Lectio is a practice with a lot of variations. One variation is to read a text four times through, focusing on identifying a different element each time: the literal meaning, an allegorical meaning, a lesson, and an action you are inspired to take.

Mandala: Producing mandalas is an Eastern practice. The way I used mandalas for this collection was by creating geometric patterns in response to the text and psychoanalyzing the product. Additionally, the process itself was a way of ensuring I could sit with the text without overthinking it.

Pardes: A Jewish exegetical practice which translates as 'orchard' but is also an acronym for the first (Hebrew) letter of each step of the approach. To practice this, identify the literal meaning, the implied meaning, an application (or choose a concept or word to study), and a hidden, mystic meaning of the text.

Prayer beads with mantra: Use words from the text as a repeated phrase and prayer beads to signal movement between

Preface

repetitions and to keep you centered. This practice is about stillness, and insights sometimes arise from that stillness.

Tarot: Tarot cards can reveal visual, symbolic insights into a text's characters or events. Tarot can also reshape the plot or provide tandem narratives to enrich the dramatic tension.

Tonglen: Buddhist nun Pema Chödrön introduces tonglen in *When Things Fall Apart*: 'Tonglen reverses the usual logic of avoiding suffering and seeking pleasure . . . We begin the practice by taking on the suffering of a person whom we know to be hurting and wish to help . . . This is the core of the practice: breathing in others' pain so they can be well and have more space to relax and open—breathing out, sending them relaxation or whatever we feel would bring them relief and happiness.' Practicing tonglen with a character in a text provides a deeper empathy for that character.

Yìjīng: A Taoist form of divination, yìjīng (or i-ching) is practiced by asking a question and throwing three coins six times. Essentially, yìjīng uses characters made from the stacking of six full or broken horizontal lines (hexagrams). The order in which the lines are combined gives the hexagram new meaning and an answer to the practitioner's question. Asking questions about an aspect of a text will garner symbols and images for poesis.

Of all the practices I encountered, I found the exegetical practices (lectio divina and pardes), the visual practices (icon meditation and tarot), and florilegium the most generative in terms of writing poetry in response to them. The exegetical practices afforded deeper logical engagement with the text and offered more complex ideas to develop. The visual practices afforded poetry with a focus on visual imagery with rich symbolism. Florilegium offered more engagement with the text of *Paradise Lost* in terms of appreciating the words of Milton at a micro level.

Preface

Final Comments

When setting out to write this collection, I wanted to retell the story of *Paradise Lost*. My intention was to produce poetry by experimenting with using sacred practices as a means of connecting to the text. It is my hope that readers of *Dying of the Light* will indeed be inspired the use contemplative practices to produce their own poetry and to seek to locate the radical challenge of śāṭān in the sacred.

Acknowledgements

THIS BOOK IS A product of my work toward a Master of Creative Writing at Auckland University of Technology, New Zealand, which passed with distinction. I want to extend my deepest thanks to my supervisor Siobhan Harvey, who saw what I saw in this project when it was in its first stages and helped me to make it real.

To the other AUT staff involved in the master's course, thank you for broadening my literary theory knowledge beyond what I thought possible. To the other candidates in my 2020 cohort, thank you for the regular Zoom catch-ups through the initial Covid-19 lockdown and beyond. The critique and conversation were invaluable, and you all inspire me with the work you are doing. Especial thanks to Andrea Malcolm for our productive critique meetings, your constant reassurance, and the opportunity to read your incredible poetry.

Thank you to my proof-reader, Patricia Bell. You kept me consistent and accurate. Thank you to John Milton for writing a generative text in *Paradise Lost*, even though I struggled with it a lot and often yelled at you for being of your time. Thank you to Vanessa Zoltan, Matt Potts, Casper ter Kuile, and Ariana Nedelman for hosting and producing *Harry Potter and the Sacred Text*, which inspired this thesis.

Poems in this collection have been previously published or shown in *The Distāntia Project, Live Encounters, Otoliths, Outer Space Inner Minds,* and *Time Capsule.* Thank you to the editors of these projects for giving my poems their first homes.

Finally, I would like to acknowledge the help of Hilary Willett. Thank you for your opinions, ideas, and feedback, but above all else, thank you for your encouragement and your boundless love and care for me.

Prologue

At the Beginning of a Journey

> *Whāia te iti kahurangi,*
> *ki te tuohu koe,*
> *me he maunga teitei.*[1]

I stand before a watchful mount, and to the lake below
I bleed my waters—this treasure for which I strive is justice.
I am here to tell your story, but I can only begin by sitting
down and listening—and giving up. I am winter dawn, late
to rise—the wild ducks and turnips marvel at the camellia
flowers decaying outside my study. I am becoming
a desolate dusk—the River of Heaven sparkles on the dew frost
on the way to the altar. Often, I wonder whether I should pluck
a few leaves and dry them—it would not poison me to drink
their tannic tea. Through divination, I discover that two travelers
cannot make a friend—in the distance, a chapel bell peals.
My wife and I are travelers—and our friend, the Church, is caught
peering through the peaceful study window. Ah! A crossroads,
I carry hard prayer beads on my wrist—while the knotweed grows.
Silence is better here. I read about you as a genderless prince
settling into a quiet place. I too decrease. I relinquish
my vocation—and give myself to the lake.

---

1. Pursue that thing of great value; if you submit, be it to a lofty mountain.

Act One

All is not lost; the unconquerable Will,
And study of revenge, immortal hate,
And courage never to submit or yield:
And what is else not to be overcome?

—*PARADISE LOST (1.106–109)*

Which way I flie is Hell; my self am Hell;
And in the lowest deep a lower deep
Still threatning to devour me opens wide,
To which the Hell I suffer seems a Heav'n.
. . .
Disdain forbids me, and my dread of shame
Among the Spirits beneath, whom I seduc'd
With other promises and other vaunts
Then to submit, boasting I could subdue
Th' Omnipotent.

—*PARADISE LOST (4.75–78, 82–86)*

Like Any Other Day

lightning strikes—	the tower—	is made—
rising from the bedrock—	raw tourmaline—	jutting up and out—
cutting malice—		
the clouds descend—	into the flame—	and deposit you—
in fiery blue and red—	the light-prince and—	in blue—
your knave—		
falling—	as the tower—	rises like clockwork—
o! the shame—	of pentacles—	nailed like—
ninety-five theses—	torn from the door—	
o! that hard work—	each disc disparaged—	
in fire—	into smoldering lake—	the ultimate death—
bleed out dear prince—		the sky turns black—
as more spirits—	sweet—	former messengers—
fall—	fall—	fall—
and accept—	prince and knave—	powerlessness—
tread the harsh wind—	red cloak fading—	past the stained-glass—
ceiling—		hem charring—
tread on—		tread on—

Why I Listen to Folk-Punk

Verses: D Bm G D Asus4 A x2
Chorus: D G D G D A x2

Deep in a desolate place, I wonder if I can find
any point to this hanging around?[1]
Heaven was not good enough for us; we never seemed to fit:
just a bunch of punks, pissed off and in love.[2]

So, I scream out to the rest that it is time to get up;
I have a plan to get us to be better.[3]
Because there is trouble in the streets, trouble never sleeps;
there is trouble running deep, so let us find it![4]

*"Fight dirty, fight dirty," that is what he said
after seven pints of beer and thirty cigarettes.*[5]
And he planted in us evil, and that evil, it has grown;[6]
we are children, one and all, of vengeful fathers.[7]

---

1. Defiance Ohio, Condition 11:11.
2. Ghost Mice, Fuck Shit Up.
3. Frank Turner, Get Better.
4. Ghost Mice, Fuck Shit Up.
5. Guignol & Mischief Brew, Fight Dirty.
6. Harley Poe, What's a Devil to Do?
7. Spoonboy, Stab Yer Dad.

Get out of the fire, kids; we will make it through this year.[8]
Burn down all the earth with your anxieties and fears.
Keep on loving, keep on fighting,[9] because
    they are going to sing your name.[10]
We were born to live and sing and dance and fight.[11]

"Fight dirty, fight dirty," that is what he said
after seven pints of beer and thirty cigarettes.
And he planted in us evil, and that evil, it has grown;
we are children, one and all, of vengeful fathers.

Yes, I am a pacifist, but I want to set fire to
what makes you comfortable; to spit back
    what we were fed from you.
Kick down your podium and never let things get this bad again.[12]
If I am not in hell, well, it might just be heaven.[13]

Because I fight dirty, fight dirty, that is what I do
every time I witness what this institution does to you:
it tries to make us bad, bad people, but we grow hope instead,
and we will keep on fighting until the day that we are dead.

---

8. The Mountain Goats, This Year.
9. Ramshackle Glory, Your Heart is a Muscle the Size of Your Fist.
10. Sledding with Tigers, The Kids Will Be Alright, Eventually.
11. Wingnut Dishwashers Union, Urine Speaks Louder Than Words.
12. Not Half Bad, Armchair Anarchism.
13. AJJ, Bad Bad Things.

Broken

In another time, the dead of night is quiet. Your skin
prickles with embarrassment. But a whispered voice—
your own—tells you it is not your fault. It is there,
downstairs on that hideous shag carpeting. Vinyl
walls reflect no sound—the world is suspended.
Figures on the muted TV dance or race or swirl
into one unending blur, unnoticed. It is not your fault.

You are just a kid at this point; who could blame you
now, as an adult? You gather your armies; you tear
apart a family. They call you harsh and ancient names.
But surely it is not malicious. Surely, it is not your fault.

Liberation I: Wrath

I breathe in a field of sunflowers I dedicate to my dead father—
a man who thought himself a god (or the other way around).

There is something in the way the light catches
these modest plants that makes me think of him.

He once told me that male, power, and God were all one,
and I was young enough to believe in him and his teaching.

He held a scepter in a meaty hand and used it to grind me down.
Strike, strike. The jewels were roughly cut. They left their mark.

He imprinted maleness onto me, and I tried to find a way out.
But then he gifted me a promise—and sealed it with a bow:

he said that one day he would lay down that bloody scepter
and crush it with his foot. One day: when I became a man.

Liberation II: For a Moment

A breath meditation in a seminary

I

As I walk through those familiar brick archways
and past that polished plaque, I think of you.
I take your frigid face in my hands
and touch your forehead with mine.

I inhale through my nostrils
and share your breath:
the cold and cloistered
space that you inhabit.

I pull out your pain with it and breathe
into you an embrace like a hearthside rug.
I let you go and stride away, unblinking.

II

And in the dying rose garden where you slept
to get away from it all—I meet you there
on the rotten bench among the agapanthus.

I pluck the noble, quiet eyes from you
and kiss them in my cupped hands.
And they become eyes of fire.

We sit on the bench for some time,
and I forget to breathe for anyone else.

Trapped, Observed

And spiral, spiral in—to the soft
purples and pinks of watercolor
inks found in old highlighters.
Vivid swirls and carefully planted
lines made by an amateur. Rose-round
like a certain cathedral. Hastily-hinted
domes or petals and a bold attempt
at symmetry. There is a secret
to where it starts—new life

where violets bloom among verdant
fields in a uniquely stained-glass sky.
And an eye repeated over jail bars
and sunsets. A panopticon.

And maybe one day, I will find
some comfort in the soft purples
and pinks that keep me captive
with their warm words
and terrible theologies.

Liberation III: Lest We Celebrate[1]

Over an ancient city, fly past spires and bell-towers;
dive into a certain square: see a mounted man sentenced
for open war. And horse, rearing, half on foot, half-flying—frozen
as if by shock, having borne witness to those coasts of dark

destruction. And the man, arm outstretched, sullen blade raised
in victorious conquest, and bright emblazonry—O!
the pride of colonial wealth. The strength of those calves—
on both horse and man, would they withstand

a sledgehammer? I swing into those defined cheekbones,
and smash the marble into a snowy dusk. I swing
again, again; tears streaming. Children bring toboggans
and mittens, and living sapphires appear to dance in the snow.

---

1. Found phrases taken from *Paradise Lost*.

Act Two

Attractive, human, rational, love still;
In loving thou dost well, in passion not,
Wherein true Love consists not; love refines
The thoughts, and heart enlarges, hath his seat
In Reason, and is judicious, is the scale
By which to heav'nly Love thou maist ascend,
Not sunk in carnal pleasure, for which cause
Among the Beasts no Mate for thee was found.

—*PARADISE LOST (8.587–594)*

Then feed on thoughts, that voluntarie move
Harmonious numbers; as the wakeful Bird
Sings darkling, and in shadiest Covert hid
Tunes her nocturnal Note.

—*PARADISE LOST (3.37–40)*

A Rare Scene

A winged refugee, alone.

Fresh blades of desert grass,
wilting gently in sympathy—
dew drops rising to kiss your eyes.

Colossus shrunk
like doubt facing
the starless void
of an infinite future.

And a deep yearning
for connection.

Ribbons and Naked Fabric

In a basket, slashing clouds in half,
is an army of angels, cooing around that kid.
They give the child flower-crowns
for a deeply poetic reason.

And I am here, guarding it all.

I am a shield, a shackled section of skin;
I let everyone know that I am owned.
That I am deeply loved. That I belong,
inescapably, to the infant-king.

No wonder you left.

And from my vantage point,
I look down and see you and remember.
This is the very moment that our mother
sends you those damned stairs as a gift to taunt you.

But I never knew who sent that opalescent lake to catch them.

Maybe you have someone on your side
after all. Maybe there is no reason
to hide your face among
those slender and delicate muscles.

Disclosure

I wash my hands in smoke and water, my face and feet
in preparation to lift the veil and see
the reality of realities—this great essence.
There is no brick without fire, so why not become all fire?
I part it with my hand and see a scene, I hear a sweet voice:
there is no place for arrogance here.
And another voice, the same, but more authoritative:
we do not use that kind of behavior in this family.
You feel attacked. Banished. Like you do not belong.
You thought you could push—that it would help—
somehow—to make them see—to spread the countless cloths
of light and dark—others have done this differently.
Your family is not so different from any other.
You thought you could defend your freedom, your boundaries,
that you might even earn their respect?
But you have been replaced. And you have lost them.
And sure, you are older and made of fire,
and they are just memories of clay,
but do you not deserve to be recognized?
There is no place for that kind of thinking here.
No place for that kind of justice.
No place for multiple justices.

A Younger Sibling Appears

They never made you clothes from scratch or houses
in the trees; they never seemed to show you love at all.
Once (while I was hiding in a nearby shrub), I saw them
make a shelter for somebody else: a brand-new child.
O! you saw that? They gathered sticks and stitched them fast
together, and sewed skins into the finest garments. What dicks.
Now, broken, you crawl—you become the serpent for the child
to crush, and you learn not to depend on parental love.
You seek out your own lumber and make your own clothes
from all your layers of shedding skin.

Wild Shelter

I keep notebooks of poetry, as most poets do,
and sometimes I look back through them.
When I do, I often stop to wonder
what compelled me to scrawl
on double-page spread
in thick red marker
I hate cicadas.
I remember why
as I sit under a perfect tree
not long after meeting an arboreal god.
I remember that I cannot record an album in March.
The cicadas infect every silence. The tūī and pīwakawaka too.
But here, under this tree, they provide a calming soundscape.
This tree shelters me with brilliant leaves of diversity
and everywhere I look, I see someone new.
They confront me with their difference.
Here, against the trunk, I become
the dust, the dirt, the many,
the utterly scattered.
I reach out.
I reach out into the throats,
and the eyes, and the nostrils.
I reach and long to be experienced.
I melt into the soil and spread, grow legs,
and rise. I push out, in groans of birth pangs
to release leaves. They feed me with tears and stories.
One day I will die, and become once more the dust, the dirt.
But now I breed kōkako and kererū in my limbs
and give wild shelter to tired strangers.[1]

    1. Tūī, pīwakawaka, kōkako, and kererū are manu (birds) of Aotearoa.

Canticle I: The Oasis

A meditation on Song of Songs

She smiles—O! she smiles—and the world
lights up anew with that graceful brilliance
of the host of heaven's stars.

The deer bounds between me
and the oasis where she drinks, unsure
which of her great thirsts she wants
to quench the most. But I see
her eyes—like a tigress—make her choice.

The waters run, a pure, clear spring,
with woody, earthen scent—and she
stops and slowly turns, but only partially—
what is it that she offers me, what does she beg me see?

I hear a rhythmic rapping coming
from the cedar tree, and wonder—should I let him in?
I have nothing to fear—for on the table
by the mirror sit the choicest fruits,
picked for a painter
or for me, for sweet devouring.

And in the vineyard, tangled mess, I see
beyond the growth, a wild fox,
a darting frenzy,
losing his control, playing first among

the hills where milk and honey mingle,
dripping leisurely
at first and then
licking his lips—

       with dual hands pressed
       and deepened gazing,
       she asks me what I need—I know
       she needs what I need too. She told me
       of the fire burning deep within her chest, she told me
       of the throbbing that is keeping her from sleep.

       This tigress-doe bends down
       to me and bows her precious head,
       and raises it, and stands up tall,
       and looks me in the eye.

Ah, I open freely in the field
of mandrake flowers. Above I see a canopy
of pomegranate trees. An arm becomes
a pillow, or a beckoning for closeness.

That sly and cunning fox is lost
amidst the tousled trap.

He pushes head to copal tree, and smells
the fragrance there,
and takes the fruit I gave to him,
and puts it to his lips.

Creation Hymn

Creation cries with all its heart—the mild melody of the graceful meadowlark, drowned by that tendermost trickle of the cursive creek. Sing, O! ocean's flow and ebb—crash into the soft sand and form the mud that makes me. I am your product, I melt and drip from you, and praise you, universal dark and light. I splatter on and seep into the cracked clay earth, and leave my impress. I am formed in reverse. Sing, O! tealight flame—prick me with joyous burns. Creation bursts at the seams and wounds its hip and echoes along the forbidden valley where children used to burn. Sing, O! wind—dance and lift all nature with you, circle, tear, and chase, chill to the bone. I am the clouds—vaporous and inconstant, fed by the lakes, lifted by love, sustained by the will of nature. So, sing! Sing, O! creation—cry out with praise as I rain myself back to you.

Dinner Plans

In a cool clearing, bottled inside a warm and dry
wood, we lounge—boughs become jungle-gyms
and cascading drapes—stripped bare of everything
but our admiration for each other. The wind twists
and crests and crashes. Ah, an intruder—or guest—
I leave to prepare cannelloni. Fresh pumpkin steamed
above tomato sauce; we have no sage in the garden—
ricotta and day-old spinach blended with the pumpkin—
but there is no piping gun. With a cheeky cabernet
and an icing spatula, I stuff the mixture, deep, deep down—
I have a secret! Some wine found itself in the sauce. I lie
them down in neat rows and cover them with the secret
sauce—the outside is, of course, perfect, but the inside—
what a mess! But I bake them in a clay oven and serve them.

Hospitality[1]

At a table under a tree, they sit, with feet on golden footstools, waiting to hear some history, and sharing a meagre meal. The house and mountain ask the tree, how were we made? The tree sighs warmly in response, once you existed as one being, yearning for diversity, so I took you, and split you, and led you to each other. And when you saw each other, I wove you together once more, and you held each other tight, and uttered whispered pleas to never leave. I gave you two fruits that you might fall deeper in love than any angry god or angel could. And one day, I will join you in the flesh, for I want to feel what you feel. But in your diversity, you noticed difference, and you called it bad. You began to fear and hate, and I knew that, when the time was right, I would put it all on—the good and the bad—to love you.

---

1. After Rublev's *Trinity*.

Act Three

With Plant, Fruit, Flour Ambrosial, Gemms & Gold,
Whose Eye so superficially surveyes
These things, as not to mind from whence they grow
Deep under ground, materials dark and crude,
Of spiritous and fierie spume, till toucht
With Heav'ns ray, and temperd they shoot forth
So beauteous, op'ning to the ambient light.
These in thir dark Nativitie the Deep
Shall yield us pregnant with infernal flame . . .

—*PARADISE LOST (6.475–483)*

But what will not Ambition and Revenge
Descend to? who aspires must down as low
As high he soard, obnoxious first or last
To basest things. Revenge, at first though sweet,
Bitter ere long back on it self recoiles;
Let it; I reck not, so it light well aim'd,
Since higher I fall short, on him who next
Provokes my envie, this new Favorite
Of Heav'n, this Man of Clay, Son of despite,
Whom us the more to spite his Maker rais'd
From dust: spite then with spite is best repaid.

—*PARADISE LOST (9.168–178)*

Finding Process

Way down, at the center of it all,
there is a ball of pure ash and fire—
and deep inside is "creating."
    Outward and outward still
    this process moves—whistling
    and groaning on its return.
        The ash feeds the fire—
        and the fire gives new life
        to the ash.
            The fire ripples out to the stars—
            and gives dust and warmth
            to the worlds.
        We drown ourselves in water
        and give attention to the cold—
        and still we recognize the dust in ourselves.
    Yet so rarely do we see
    the fire in ourselves—
    so seldom are we complete.
So rarely do we see
the very center of it all—
so seldom do we see the change.

Aroha Mai, Aroha Atu[1]

From the chariot, unfathomable oceans of fragrant petals part
like a dish-soap finger in a bowl of pepper-water—and one
by one, I take three petals to shape the cosmic immensity,
the patulous sky, the adamant. They shift and circle each other
and take on new life. I embody the earth and become all humanity.
Split in equal parts. I am the life. I unhide all things. I take creating
and make it my path. I am lotus petals, defined also by my own
absence. I make you all lotus petals that shift and circle each other
and take on new life. When I die, I am resurrected. The petal in me
drifts on the updraft to join the mass. My knowledge and experience
become public consciousness and then—some of us fall
at different paces, we are differently eager. But we all shift
and circle each other, and take on new life.

---

1. Love received, love returned.

Bugle

The clouds divide for this—the waters still. Daggers
are plunged deep into the earth and all creation turns
to watch. The cups are mixed; the alchemist breathes
and puffs, and tufts—great bursts of smoke—erupt
in a handsome twist and rise in ribbons.

And all at once, arms outstretched,
like a surrendered infant hearing trumpet's call,
it is created. Standing, outlooking—grasp that tree,
that wand and look: all creation—all creation breathes too.

The Birth of Institutions

Out in the desert, the lush green erupts, dancing out of nothing, opening out into the harsh sun, calming the wind, springing water into mouths of cracked dirt. And spiraling into being is a woman, tender and soft-spoken; she would drown herself for her narcissism. She rises to a voice and it leads her to a man, tall and broad-shouldered. His hair is perfect. Breast presses against chest in the great embrace. His ecstaticity matches hers: he is glad she will witness his glory.

You see this and find it disturbing: a relic of the patriarchy. Yet part of you is jealous of imagined perfection. You hear "beauty" and fall into small desolations as you visualize unrealistic body sizes.

A Bowl of Fruit

Filtered sun rays land soft on the painting. Each graceful and delicate beam glistens, illuming the texture of each insistent, steady stroke. Whisking, slapping harsh crimsons liberally, stained skin and wet brushes pushed into firm canvas. Stretched tension, threatening to burst, bound on the very edge. Slight touches start to show dimples and spaces to be filled. The pale gives way to color as the sun continues to watch. Sheer layers upon layers, pressed together. One, two—one, two. With a small surprise slipped in, shifting in the changing light, seeming to glow, O! now the senses are brimming. The colors are coming together, combining. Swirling and flowing free and unified and . . .   the image is finished.
The artist is now a spectator, savoring the fresh waves of meaning pulsating from the work, guzzling new ideas and inspiration, delighting in the radiance of the art.
The rays of light dance slower on the canvas as if they too are sated.

Bricks Fall

I

Arms in orans, flame for hair, the two stand below,
freshly created. Gently depicted with bellybuttons—
ah! the truth for natural selection or chance, tenderly
hidden within generations of art. In this gallery,
I view and meditate. A mountain in the background
is too much resistance against the earth. One day,
as with everything, it shall fall.

II

One day, it shall all become chaotic water. Lions
and lizards bow to this force and decay, returning
everything to everything. Prosperity shines
upon these two for now. I sit on a bench and wonder
how much entropy a rainbow has. The world
and all four living creatures are a wreath tied
together with rough red cloth. And this too shall decay.

The Great Plot

I take a walk through an orchard. The ground is wet; the air is clean. The mud is already caked onto my jeans. And in the dense foliage, I see a cloud descending like a cherub on a map, but fierce and livid. The leaves part and down comes a prismatic sanctuary, glimmering with robust, burning buttresses and triumphant banners draped along the sides. In the middle sits a flaming figure, contemplating as though that be its native state, unblinking and unmoving, the utter, perfect god. It talks, I think I hear, unless that is a visitor, I see so many visitors go up and down the throne. I see a child. Meek and calm, lost among the angels. It seems to know that something is beginning. It appears to be in armor—no, it cannot be. They seem to be plotting—maybe a war—against an invented enemy that they have brought into existence to glorify that kid. The clouds regather, and I find the fruit in my hand soured at its plucking. The mud has risen to my chest and climbs—as if with all the time in the world—to my face.

Baptized First in Blood

Harsh and wicked cutting—gather up the dreadful dirt,
fling mountains, march maliciously—at this crucial moment,
the seething leaks and drips and forms a torrent
of speckled light and dancing dust motes.

Tossed, cast! Horse and rider heaved into the sea,
crushed under wheel and made immaterial—
forced to slither on the road to the end
through a tear in the very fabric.

And one with eyes of fire rises above—
the fighting stops and both sides stare:
darkening clouds assemble, a lofty scowl
scatters onlookers with needles of love.

Tough Love

When you were nine, you discovered that there was only one way
to learn. Until then, you had grand notions of varied pedagogy,
of inquiry—ones that opened doors, made willing kids, had room
for you. But then you were nine and the whip cracked and you
learned the truth: forgiveness is for chumps and Christians. You heard
it said, an eye for an eye, but I tell you: carry out those personal
vengeances, let them rot you to the core, be like your Maker
in heaven and rely on champagne warring. When you were nine,
you were beaten. Crushed into the small dust, and compressed
into charcoal bricks and used for toasting incense. You were a big
kid. There was no excuse for your actions, but you fought back. You
had guts. You built a mighty machine made of the most insulting
gunmetal, aimed, and promptly fired. And somewhere in the fight,
the world burned ivory, and you saw That Grim Parent in younger
skin raging toward you. You ran up the stairs and hid. Had you heard
that voice before? Had you ever felt yourself jerked from the closet
and flung down the stairs, far from your room? When you hit
the floor, you turned ten. No-one ever grew up so fast. You used
to believe in willing kids—that kids could change—
that you could take your behavior, externalize it, talk about it, take
it to a new place, change it. But now creation is not so colorful.
You have become the destroyer of worlds.

Alone Time

you and I are
under the bed

hiding beneath
the dark and cozy

the blankets
bring comfort

pressed into
clothes

a coat closet
and precarious icicles

stale
shallow breath

in a chest
anywhere

an old icebox
small enough

a large drawer
to hide

but do not return to
tattered shreds

the closet
and broken glass

you will find
where you were

Streetlight

It is late—you can hear the cosmos wheezing, the bass rumbles
of freight trains and distant traffic. The moon, like a vet
        or pre-school teacher,
laughs kindly. Softly. But the moon, the stars, and the cool, crisp air
know that midnight is a time for decision-making,
        for big life choices.
You have never known a city road to feel so safe.
        When you have nothing
to lose—when you have nowhere to go—anywhere
        can become home.
You look longingly at a flower, crumpled and tossed, forgotten.
        And wonder
when you will next see such delicate colors,
        or such strong symmetry.
I think your face is the bravest I have ever seen.
        I really admire how your suitcase
makes that rittle-rattle-rittle-rattle on the pavement;
        it makes you seem less alone.
This tore you. Like sourdough, not kneaded enough.
        Slowly falling apart.
Were you wanted? And still you fell apart. You are falling now.
        Down, down, down.

The Fall, Part One: Suspension

When light and dark collide, those who are both survive.
You breathe, and scrunch your face, and spit in an eye.

And mutter about hypocrisy and fling yourself
away from dark, and into the known.

Down through chaos (who will soon reclaim everything
and bides their time, patient as an unfinished bathroom).

But you will sit in chaos for a few days, give them company,
chat about the small things—work, or dinner, or time.

Eventually the shadow fades, and the underneath opens up
and swallows, and it seems to lookers-on that you are lost.

And for a moment, the world stands still
in terror, that defiance could be lost.

The Fall, Part Two: Firmly Held

I know that having courage is hard for you.
> The whole world seems to be locked away
> behind veiled doors and mirrored windows.
> The friends you made seem so far,
> even though you carry them wherever you go.

I know that you are second-guessing your choice to fall.
> Thinking things might be different if you apologize
> and take that heavy yoke of blame.
> Thinking a second chance for them
> is the same as a second chance for you.

I know that you blame yourself anyway.
> There is no shortage of things
> you could have done differently.
> But you know your family—
> do you really think they could change?

I know that you do.
> That is why you are going to do this.
> That is why you are going to stand tall,
>> brush yourself off,
>>> walk into that garden,
>>>> make the world hell.

The Fall, Part Three: Filthy Hands and Muddy Feet

Back in the garden, you watch me run my fingers
        through the flowerbeds,
those tulips and autumn daffodils springing back from my touch.
you watch me tracing slender, scented fingers on my neck.

You see me resting in the shade of my favorite wild oak.
I have tied a hammock around its middle, and there I read.
You see me fall asleep and forget all about the work of the day.

And now you walk, freshly fallen, amidst the discarded leaves,
littering the path, falling in the flowerpots, choking all the herbs.
Now you walk and mutter that there is no one here
        to wash your feet.

The Fall, Part Four: Resentment

Here you are, bare feet on the damp lawn. You cast your eyes down
and consider having it mowed. How dare it grow on your watch.
How dare it interrupt your deliberations. It has caught you
at a tricky time: you are in one of your moods.

Sometimes you are fine with taking "no"
for an answer. Sometimes you are fine
with being shown up.
Today is not one of those days.

Today is one of those inspired days.
One of those days when you could bring
the light back into the world and dazzle people
with your magnificence. With your significance.
One of those days when you could set humanity free.

And maybe, on a clear spring day such as this,
when you might have a more mischievous temperament,
there might be a hidden, sinister motive.

A voice in your head speaks to you.
It tells you to do it. To set them free.
And the grass weeps as you stride on.

The Fall, Part Five: Taste the Fruit

I plunge my fingers deep into the baked sand;
there has never been a perfect day before this one.
Somewhere, an unseen magician sprinkles glitter
over the surface of the gently rolling ocean.

You are an echo, but you could be as gods.

I lazily watch through tinted glass, music soothing
as he bounces and frolics among the waves.
His jubilant laughter reaches my ears like a beckoning finger,
But there is a storm approaching, and I do not plan to get wet.

You could undermine everything. Fix everything.

They gather quick, the clouds. Heat sucked from the earth.
Laughter is replaced by a similar sound. Panic.
A call, and an impulse to do something rash washes over me
and I find myself under the water, lost.

You could have dominion, let the world serve you.

I swim. Fast as I can, but he seems to be caught,
drifting, further out. Beyond my reach. Gone.
Until—my fingers meet flesh, lips on salty shoulder,
tears meet in relief—we are not safe, but we are together.

You could remake the world in your image.

He names me. Like an animal. Stands over me and rises
on the crest of a wave and up. Rises into the stars and among the moon.
His eyes glow piercing white and a horde of voices speak from his lips:
I will never again be one with you. This is my world now.

Act Four

This would surpass
Common revenge, and interrupt his joy
In our Confusion, and our Joy upraise
In his disturbance; when his darling Sons
Hurl'd headlong to partake with us, shall curse
Thir frail Original, and faded bliss,
Faded so soon.

—*PARADISE LOST (2.370–376)*

Over the foaming deep high Archt, a Bridge
Of length prodigious joyning to the Wall
Immovable of this now fenceless world
Forfeit to Death; from hence a passage broad,
Smooth, easie, inoffensive down to Hell.

—*PARADISE LOST (10.301–305)*

Optimism

The very ground is cursed. But when my fist
bursts through the cracks, and I ascend,
dragging with grasping claws, I breathe
the first saintly sigh, and all nature sings
in me. The ground is cursed, but my womb
erupts with life-giving blood and all the earth
grows flowers and bitter herbs.

Canticle II: A Grove

A break in trust and eyes aside, shame settles swift on them:
now timid yet impatient, he boasts inflated pride; and with eyes
of toxic fire, she spreads her ardor out. Drink greedily of crystal cup,
take it to lips with force. He will not be satisfied if he looks only inward.
She will walk away tonight, foiled of her thrill.

He saddens when he realizes the chase
was a better thrill and so he plans to emulate:
sees flowers and plucks them and ties their stems together

and binds two arms inward. An external person is controlling his pride
with her wiles, the feminine charm, this unknowable force—
he will learn to control it, or learn to cope without.

She used to play a gender that she has now thrown out—
a meek—a humble housewife concerned with another's thrill
while denying the potency of her flirtatious force.

And as of men, the pleasure to know them alludes her, except for one,
yet now, her body is her source of pride—
is she a Madonna honest or harlot, muddy inward?

There is subtle hate that he holds in hardened heart inward:
a self-important hoggish need that he, with haste,
thrusts out with all earnest expectation she will serve his pride and tickle will,
and meet his needs, and give him double thrills.

And yet he knows these thrills are not how he imagines them.
If not served, he prepares to take what he needs now by force.

She has learnt a subtler way: there is only so much force can do,
so she attacks where he cannot see: in that inward place
where broken feelings torture—he is overcome with them.

She has learnt what strings to pull and how to play her gender out.
She has learnt a secret way to power: submit to him
and thrill him where he asks, snakish manipulation, please his pride.

A break in trust and eyes aside—averted from the other's pride.
There is a pleasure where their bodies play. Some fun in their force.
Some pleasure in the newness, an unrestrained thrill.

They both look out with eyes of glass and cold hearts kept inward.
Yet there is an acknowledgement of other: looking out.
They say they are getting what they want. Pity them.

It is not the fault of pride, or locked emotions inward,
but the force of the great and terrible fall, casting out
the security, that thrill—cursing fragility on them.

Like That Other Day

I
Storm clouds gather,
the lightning strikes
        once more—
there is no greater law.

II
The galaxy twists—
the tower will crumble
as the sky and earth re-join.

III
An unchaste glance,
penetrative stare—
the universe unfolds

IV
Everything will fall
together—the bluebird's
song will cease.

Death

enters the world to dine and sup. Slowly—
steadily—with no need to gorge or glut. She takes
the refuse out. She keeps the glimmer on the water-top,
milks the toxins—gone. She has an energy—calm
and constant—when you get to know her, but—oh dear!
She is not the kind of girl to bring home to the family. She is wild.

Now is the time for the earth to rest—to take a year
of Jubilee. She stops that damned decay from spreading
its roots, and instead begins a process of renewal.
She is a welcome friend after all this turmoil—
she is a hellhound of God, and when she follows
you everywhere, that is God saying you are loved.

Death is becoming Mother Nature—trees grow around
her as she paces. Soft rabbits parade around her throne
before they wither back to the ground. She sucks the water
from flowers and watches them wilt.

On a Bench, Observing a Bridge

Are the flowers cold yet?—Seashells are
carried by the songs of frogs and skylarks.
The mist covers the moon, reminding us

to wear more clothes—but the ground strips
itself of snow. The forgotten frost creeps—
the laughing mountain increases in flower

buds. Air conditioners leak water that trickles
off rocks and feeds moss—the rainbow speaks
to lost promises. Autumn-has-come is here—

the typhoon crosses the bridge, lanterns
extinguish and hope leaves for shelter.
In winter, trees are lost—the breath is visible.

All coldness crosses the aging bridge—
even the mountain sleeps while the lone
wolf keeps his vigil for another year.

A Mountain Landscape[1]

The fierce wind strips the tree—and leaves become dust.
A family set apart from the amber hue of stormtime encroaching,
and a mule that smells danger. People hauling sodden nets
on one knee, like digging a grave or saying evening prayers.

There is a town, a tower, a mountaintop, and all become dust.
A dress for dancing and hair tied up, her arm twists
as though the wind has swept all hope from her hand
and maybe she could still catch it before it leaves.

The waterfall comes crashing down, it too becomes dust.
The other fishers catch the eye of the woman on the rock;
she worries that all they see is her child, that she is insufficient.
She is as sufficient as the leaves and town and waterfall.

The woman and her child, the dog, and the men—they become dust.
The sky turns from pale peach to baby blue before following suit,
the birds take wing and find nowhere to settle, and slowly,
like a crawl, the world, each soul and body turns to dust.

---

1. After Vernet's *A Mountain Landscape with an Approaching Storm.*

Institutions

I let them in, for they are all I need:
a mighty mountain littered with flowers.
And so I follow, follow where they lead.

They promise, by commitment, I am freed
to enter their adamantine tower.
I let them in, for they are all I need.

While I am in, I watch the others bleed,
and weep for their souls another hour.
And so I follow, follow where they lead.

I swear to them my words, I swear my deeds.
Since honest hearts never become sour,
I let them in, for they are all I need.

I turn a cheek when confronted with greed.
Surely greed is but a sign of power,
and so I follow, follow where they lead.

But on this hillside, I see only weeds,
where once I saw soft and fragrant flowers.
I let them in, for they are all I need.
And so I follow, follow where they lead.

Reflection

You have seen the fruit. It dropped from your hand
and shattered the earth. Voices erupted from the cracks.
You hear the laughter coming from a distant chariot
and wonder if you could feel less like a pawn.
This fruit grows roots and spreads. It becomes a rare tree.

Did this callow commotion change the way your family
feels about you? I see you set your face in your palms
and I wonder why you thought rebellion would lead
to acceptance. But you never thought that, did you?
You were hurt. You did not care. You never saw these fruits.

Act Five

Michael from Adams eyes the Filme remov'd
Which that false Fruit that promis'd clearer sight
Had bred; then purg'd with Euphrasie and Rue
The visual Nerve, for he had much to see;
And from the Well of Life three drops instill'd.
So deep the power of these Ingredients pierc'd,
Eevn to the inmost seat of mental sight,
That Adam now enforc't to close his eyes,
Sunk down and all his Spirits became intranst:
But him the gentle Angel by the hand
Soon rais'd, and his attention thus recall'd.

—*PARADISE LOST (11.412–422)*

The World was all before them, where to choose
Thir place of rest, and Providence thir guide:
They hand in hand with wandring steps and slow,
Through Eden took thir solitarie way.

—*PARADISE LOST (12.646–649)*

Future I: Cain and Abel

Tall grass sways and parts to my foot—such hard work
to climb, panting, to the great hilltop. But when I arrive,
I can see paradise and all creation, spread out before me
like a vulnerable lover. I want to take it all in, but an angel
strips my eye and drops some liquid in—my eyes clamp shut—
and they tenderly stroke my arm to find my hand. Fingers
interlace and I am led, firm and sure. So I submit—they take
me there. At a whisper in my ear, my eyes release, expand,
and through the smoky glass I see an uninterrupted field—
a relentless summer's day, and an unresisted arrest. I see
a knee plunged into a neck beside a cop car.

And in the yellow haze I know it is fear that drove the car,
and the adversary who carried pickets and candles silently.
The very ground weeps in sympathy—I tell my angel
that it is not fair, but the angel merely watches.
I become the adversary.

Future II: Noah's Lullaby

Sleep, son, your day is done. The greying sky remains
to watch your body wither and uphold your legacy.
A brilliant bow arcs wide across open terrain:
a promise that our dear friend death will one day cease to be.

Ah, death. I see now, you were a sign of love:
a tool to teach, but not enforce, lessons of self-control.
I know all influence descends from high above,
and through you is the only way to reach my greatest goal.

I sing for freedom from the tyranny of life:
I say goodbye to tempting times. I say goodbye to war.
I say goodbye to both my happiness and strife.
Goodbye to all the luxuries of flesh I had before.

And so, I close my eyes and hear the flood of tears
drown all of humanity, the terror and screaming fear.
Through the smoke, my son lives on, throughout every year,
until one dove returns to declare that all the skies are clear.

Future III: Overheard at a Seminary

It was the devil that brought postmodernity into the world
and shattered objective truth with distrust and disbelief
at Babel—that is how I read it anyway.

Surrender

I

There is a volunteer. One of those helper-types
who wants to take away the suffering;
one of those pain-avoidant people.

But when he is bravely born into a male skin,
taking on transgender identities,
he will bear all the burn and bite of broken families.

He will come out from the fabric of the universe to say
that we are doing some stuff okay,
To tell us to throw away the rules of redemption
and let our hearts decide how honest we are.

II

But—and I am sure he knows—there will be a new empire established
by a slippery saboteur who will build barriers and barricades
(like all good empires have). It will keep the people out (or in).

The people will think themselves the heroes—align themselves
    with friends,
and ignore what they were taught about enemies.
They shall fight on the beaches, in the streets, and in the churches.

And the ultimate enemy—who tricked them all—will receive
    the least love.
And they will never admit to the enemy's salvation, nor each other's.
And they will walk out of this world into the warmth
    of breaking structure
and into the ever-changing center, and forget that they ever cared.

III
One day, those walls will fall, and we will see the volunteer again.
His eyes will crease and mouth will widen, and he will ask
what took us so long. We will be welcomed into a skin-tight
    embrace.
All because the Church returned to dust, and to God.

End

You storm the streets with your energetic anthem:
"fight dirty, fight dirty," but you forget
that someone else taught it to you.

And it is not until, amid the tear gas and screams,
you hear the enemy chant that same, haunting rhythm,
and you feel your bones turn to liquid, and your skin to scales,
that you know you are utterly rejected.

These new protesters riot against you;
they have put on your mantle.
They have become the śāṭān.

Wood and Water

As the incense rises, so do my prayers. As the candles
burn, so does my soul. Here, I find community
between the wood and water. If not in hanging muslin,
Taizé chants, or shared silence, I find it nestled firmly
between food and font. If not in soft, slow reading,
four times through, in icons, or chimes, I find it dancing
in all that space between bread and baptism, cross
and christening. If not in people laughing or sharing
favorite recipes, if not the stories of each other
that we already know, if not the singing and listening
and watching we do together, I find community
between the sacred wood and water.

Unlike Any Other Day

the spirit descends—	the church—	is born—
rising from the mud—	raw spiritual empire—	loving—
hastily—		
the smoke thickens—	around my eyes—	and I see—
a child king (sacrificed)—	manipulated by—	a generation—
of me—		
falling as—	the church—	rises—
o! the shame of—	empiric might—	boasted like—
anarchy—	like communism—	
a crying man—	voiceless—	the ultimate death—
in fire—		
bleed out dear prince—	into the arms—	of smiling strangers—
become universal truth—	of pain—	and bitterness—
rise—	rise—	rise—
deny—		powerlessness—
withstand harsh wind—	and ventriloquism—	of the stained-glass—
and scolding sermons—	crown released—	and sceptre fallen—
be still—	be still—	descend the mountain—

Felix Culpa

The time has come to tread through warring trees;
step lightly on the recent-fallen leaves.
Bid goodbye to handsome home of late.
Walk on, walk on, walk through the garden gate.

Leave behind the glow of crystal spring,
the lushness of the lawn, the birds on wing.
Walk into the barren desertscape,
and think this as your permit to escape.

More dignity you carry as you leave,
though just as much loss for you to grieve
than the enemy who suffered above all;
though both, through time, become a happy fall.

Epilogue

Onward: A Benediction

I hope reading this has served you—
has grown you in one direction or the other.
I hope you have not stayed still.
I hope reading this has challenged you in some way—
has made you question some assumptions.
I hope you go to protests.

I hope, one day, you will call me up, and tell me
that you are the śāṭān—the protester. I will say I know.
I hope you give this book to someone.
I hope you start to wonder why an angry god appeals,
      why an enemy is needed.
That God lays down God's gender in your eyes.
      That the śāṭān gives you courage.
I hope you plant some seeds.

I hope you take root in reality and spring forth,
and when you die, you return to the ground.
I hope you live well and spread joy.
I hope, when you walk out into the world,
      with the garden behind you,
you serve by uplifting the spirit of the other.

www.ingramcontent.com/pod-product-compliance
Lightning Source LLC
Chambersburg PA
CBHW071732040426
42446CB00011B/2329